Inside / Out

Inside/Out
SELECTED POEMS

Marilyn Buck

Foreword by David Meltzer

City Lights Books • **San Francisco**

Cover design by Linda Ronan

Library of Congress Cataloging-in-Publication Data
Buck, Marilyn, 1947–2010.
 Inside/out : selected poems / Marilyn Buck ; preface by David
Meltzer.
    p. cm.
 ISBN 978-0-87286-577-8
 I. Title.

 PS3552.U3337I57 2012
 811'.54—dc23

                        2012007900

City Lights Books are published at the City Lights Bookstore,
261 Columbus Avenue, San Francisco, CA 94133.
www.citylights.com

Dedicated to my mother Virginia Grace
without whom I would not have the grace
to embrace life as it comes
and
Mtyari Shabaka and Kuwasi Balagoon
embracers of life, fearless before death

CONTENTS

FOREWORD

by David Meltzer

This is a time when the world seeks revelation.
Too many seek that which is not but illusion or reassurance;
those who thirst for visions drink hallucinations.

Marilyn Buck — revolutionary, poet, artist, transla-
tor, teacher — died of uterine cancer in August 2010 at
the age of 62. Marilyn had been a political prisoner in the
U.S. federal prison system for nearly half of her life, and
she died just twenty days after being released on medical
parole. I'll forgo the history behind her extended impris-
onment since it's available on friendsofmarilynbuck.com,
along with a deeply felt tribute by her comrade Felix Shafer.
Suffice to say, she put her radical consciousness into action.

I was Marilyn's teacher as she worked toward a mas-
ters degree in poetics at San Francisco's New College of
California. It was a process that shaped itself with the in-
estimable help of New College administrator Tom Parsons
who, once the paper logistics were worked out and the
funds ascertained, constructed the plan to give Marilyn a
long-distance education. All of her required classes were
recorded on audio cassettes that Tom either mailed di-
rectly to the prison or delivered to her in person. Course
readers and handouts were mailed to her, and we hoped
they would arrive in a timely fashion and not be withheld
by the prison officials.

I taught the "context" courses, i.e., if a semester was focusing on the Romantics, my course would address the social, political, and technological impact on shaping human experience. Even in difficult circumstances, Marilyn always got her assignments done. She was a superb and exemplary student. Despite her isolation, Marilyn was an omnivorous and discerning reader. She was a clear thinker, with an ability to process my free-form lectures into lucid questions and answers. It must have frustrated her not to be able to fully participate in classroom discussion.

We began corresponding — her letters were written in a spidery cursive — and then we added occasional phone calls, which were limited for Marilyn and could last only five minutes. The first group of poems she sent were varied — ranging from occasional jots to current event politics — with some poems reflecting a deeper tone and voice — that which emerges in the works collected here.

Finally, I made my first visit to the Dublin Federal Correctional Institution with Felix Shafer and his partner, muralist Miranda Bergman. Until then, Marilyn Buck had been more of an abstraction than a real presence as a student. And even though I had worked in the prison system, I had had no idea how difficult it was for Marilyn to create within her situation.

I feel the pain of every single day here. I regret and miss the simple things — family, children, a lover, comrades, and involvement in political struggle. But after each nightmare of a day passes, it is history and I look forward to what is to come.

Miranda's driving. I'm in the front seat and Felix sits in back. We're on the freeway headed to Dublin, the federal correctional facility located on a military base. They've been visiting Marilyn for as long as she's been there. I have no idea of what to expect, but as soon as we enter the base we're checked by armed men, our ID's peered at stonily, and finally we're allowed to drive into the parking lot. We enter a waiting room with glass cases selling correction employee gear: T-shirts, hats. Rows of benches are filled with other people hoping to visit inmates. A racially and ethnically diverse group of men and women and an assortment of kids from babies to teenagers sit or stand, waiting to be processed by a husky woman officer behind a high desk. Felix brings me a paper to sign that's to be brought to the officer who sits before a computer screen. Groups of people talking, some people silent, kids awkward in the large room, except for one little girl unhinged and resisting her grandmother's embarrassed, ineffective whispers. When we get to the desk, our paper is taken, ID's turned over to the impassive officer. Everyone empties their pockets into a tray, belts are removed, keys, money, and we walk through a metal-detecting frame. Some people are also selectively rubbed by a special pad to detect traces of narcotics or explosive powders. Since I walk on crutches and have metals inside my body, I'm pulled aside, patted down and wanded by a male guard who looks like Buster Keaton. One woman is asked to leave because she's wearing beige pants — their color too close to the uniforms worn by inmates. Another is told she's wearing the wrong kind of shoes and she's not allowed entry. Once we pass the various tests and are cleared for entry, the top side of our right hands are stamped with a Chinese ideogram. The little frustrated girl is suddenly quiet for the moment. We're on line with 10 people being led through a clanking, electrically operated door. I'm told by a guard in a room with desks and other officers behind a thick glass window to put my right hand under a small black light to see if my ideogram lights up right.

Finally we're led by another guard through another thick door to a path that leads to the prison meeting area. It's a cafeteria-sized space with an outside section closed in by glass where smokers can be with their visitors, and inside, up a small flight of stairs, a glass enclosed area for kids and parents to play in. Against one wall is a bank of vending machines and a microwave. In the main room are tables and white plastic chairs. Facing everything is a raised desk overseen by three female corrections officers. Not exactly the panopticon, but it attempts to be all-seeing.

As we enter, many of the tables are filled with families, boyfriends, friends.

Most of the inmates are in for drug charges. It's clear that many of the women are doing time for their drug-dealer boyfriends or husbands. Marilyn's a minority — a political prisoner.

She enters the room in a tan uniform hobbling very slightly from a gunshot wound from the '60s. Marilyn's tall, well coiffed, wearing horn-rim glasses. Despite almost two decades of imprisonment, she is radiant and open-faced. Felix, Miranda and I start talking excitedly about current events, then switch to updates on their many comrades released and still confined. There's a direct forthrightness to Marilyn's speech; also a circumspection. Felix goes off to the vending machines, bringing back nuked popcorn and assorted goodies to our round formica-topped table. Marilyn and I begin what will become an ongoing discussion of our classes, literature, poetry, and creative resistance. While Felix and Miranda talk with Marilyn, I watch the other tables: inmates holding their children, mothers and grandmothers talking with their daughters and granddaughters. Guys talking with their imprisoned girlfriends, sometimes tentatively touching each other, holding hands, or nervously avoiding eye contact.

When the allotted three hours is over, after hurried hugs and kisses, all the people get in line on one side of the room while the inmates move together to the other side. We are let out, as we entered, in groups of 10 supervised by one of the women guards. Those moments of leaving were the saddest moments of any visit. Prisoners waving to their visitors, some blowing kisses, others trying not to cry.

Through tenacity and the reclamation of desire — our life force — the poet, and the reader, may survive — super survive — both great horrors and not-so-great traumas to truly live in this world as human beings.

On my last last visit to Marilyn, she was excited by a possible early parole date, though she knew she was already quite sick with what would be diagnosed as a rare form of uterine cancer. We talked about this book. During some earlier visits she had said she wanted to be judged not as a political prisoner poet, but simply as a poet. After her death, Felix, Miranda and I went through several stages of editing from her various manuscripts with that criterion in mind. Later, poet Jack Hirschman and publisher Elaine Katzenberger of City Lights also selected from the range of her work and helped shape the collection you see here.

Marilyn's sympathy and kinship with the oppressed and alienated was real, not merely ideological. She was constantly evolving in her political thinking, which is reflected in many of her poems. She also loved music, and music as subject appears in many of the poems, as do the lives of many of the women prisoners she taught and befriended. Her poetic inspirations were many and varied, ranging from Milton and Blake to Fanny Howe and devorah major, and including many of the Latin American poets, such as Vallejo, Neruda and Cristina Peri-Rossi. (Marilyn's translation of Peri-Rossi's *State of Exile* was published by City Lights in 2008.) She was also intrigued by haiku.

The work you are about to explore represents a wide range of Marilyn's output, written over the course of her imprisonment. From within a repressive and often cruel environment, she not only found her poetic voice, but resisted the self-negation demanded by the constant torments of a system that aims to dehumanize its subjects. She was a brave and forthright woman who spent a major portion of her life behind bars, surviving punitively repressive treatment because of her political and moral courage. She found added strength and resiliency by writing, as well as teaching her fellow prisoners: creative writing, art, yoga, counseling those who turned to her for support and guidance. Marilyn died with grace and dignity, with that clarity she always worked from. All of her work reflects this — a clarity that was enhanced, not destroyed, by decades of imprisonment.

Teaching is learning and learning is teaching. It's a circular ongoing process.

Marilyn was as much my teacher, even more so, than I was hers.

Seek not revelations, all is revealed.
Listen to each word, a world in orbit;
each phrase, a nova: essay the beach,
each grain of sand, a poem

do not sit idle, your path streams before you.
bank the raging fires and light laurel branches against the cold.

Inside / Out

PRISON

no grass
no trees
no children throwing stones
into puddles
no laughter
no tears

no peace
no silence
no world of colors
no sun
no moon
no weather at all

Living without
blowing winds
gentle rains
day or night
my internal clock
is deprived of nature's power

There is only the beat of my heart

CLANDESTINE KISSES

for Linda and her love

kisses
bloom on lips
which have already spoken
stolen clandestine kisses

a prisoner kisses
she is defiant
she breaks the rules
she traffics in contraband women's kisses

a crime wave of kisses
bitter sweet sensuality
flouting women-hating satraps
in their prison fiefdoms
furious
that love
can not be arrested

FEB. 11, 1990

we walk inside the walls
3 pairs of feet
whisper softly against cruel pavement
a cold crisp morning
the sun promises to touch us
if we stay longer

time's up
one hour
we must go
9:16 A.M.

across the sea
another continent
4:16 P.M.
the sun touches
Nelson Mandela's last footsteps
they echo off prison walls
as he passes through steel gates
into the radiance of African voices
raised in jubilation
"Mandela is free"
"Free South Africa"

the sun breaks through
inside these bars

where we too
stand in sweet company

MOON BEREFT

Beyond razor-wired walls
the moon shimmers in the late summer sky
spills over in pale brightness
to draw me into its fullness
washing my eyes in quicksilver

Now, in a heavy-lidded cell
moon-bereft nights leave me weeping
tears well up in dry cratered wounds
despair rises
dark and irradiated
to swallow starlight
and spit it out
like steel needles
that incite my loneliness

My soul careens off cell walls
wails till pain tires
and the pale moon of memory
appears to call me home

DESIRE SUITE

rainy day
restless cloaks
slow bittersweet hours
in gray

i'm captured in falling sky warmth

blue jazzy notes
slide between the rain drops
dance on my flesh
blow dreams

i pace
my robe's swish
a desire suite
sweeps across the sound barrier

i call you
from the golding gray
    place your kiss
    upon my thigh

FASHION REPORT

in the 1960's Vietnamese children
their fine-boned beauty profiled
ran down burning roads
draped in napalm

what are the children of Iraq wearing this year?
do they gleam of phosphorous in cratered ruins?
do they trail liquid-red chiffon
down the streets?

fashion editors have abandoned Baghdad
dressed in desert storm fatigues

there is no news to report

GONE

there are days when I'm gone
I do not know where I went
but I wasn't here

    that's true for me too . . .
    sometimes I'm so gone
    that maybe I wasn't ever really here

        chill you two
        you don't even know where gone is

        I know, I've been gone so long
        that here is only a state of mind
        a play on words

    Did you hear that?

No, I'm outta here!

IMPERATIVES

bring me out
mine the wild abandon
that was mine
once
when I was seventeen
a young wraith in black
bells ringing in flight
wrapped around a young man's back
on a BMW that wound up mountains
to a naked lunch
on ice-planted crags
pounded by the Pacific

once
when I was thirty
entrancing from clandestine
curtained brilliance
a subversive siren in a sea
of easily parted waves of dark-eyed lovers

awaken passion one more time
I am in danger!
the zodiac abandons me
to land-locked shadows
they smother me flat

I cannot breathe without
the vivid rainbow edge

find me
free me from pale dry days
of drab restraint

NIGHT SHOWERS

fifteen years ago
I bathed in morning's anticipation

now, after the sun drops
over the edge of the world
I hasten into showers
where water falls from walls
etched by prisoners' tears and curses

into safety I slide
fugitive from the State's eyes
alone
anointed

memory washes
the sorrow-drenched day
my spirit swirls tomorrow
into its eye
flings disappointment
down the well of yesterday

NAMES

my movement
led to a clandestine world
where *Marilyn* spoken
mustn't evoke even a startled eye
it did cause a tripping
behind my heart

I collected other names
sometimes more than one at once
some musical
some brief
useful names to be called
when others wanted my attention
or proof of identity
like scarves
draped over shoulders
decorative
concealing

on capture
an FBI man uttered
Marilyn
a question
a victory shout

named
I had no option but
    Marilyn
scarves stripped
by howling winds of retribution

JAPANESE TEA CEREMONY

Takako slips off her rayon dress
wraps in layers of cotton kimono
a ritual cocooning

the tea ceremony unfolds
an extraordinary gift
distilled and poured
into prisoners' cups of sorrow

THIRTEEN SPRINGS

had you planted a tree
to fill in the deep well
of my absence
that tree would be
thirteen springs high
high enough to relieve
the relentless sun of incarceration
strong enough to bear
the weight of children
who might have been born
had I not been seized
from your life and plunged
into this acid-washed crypt
of perpetual loss
and high-wired vigilance

but there is no tree
that stands in my place
to harbor birds and changing winds
perhaps someone will plant
a willow   a eucalyptus
or even a redwood
any tree that will
in thirteen years more
bear fruit and provide shelter

WOMAN WITH CAT AND IRIS

three purple iris
poised among crystal dew
morning-blurred sun
back drops black birds
flickering across day canvas
raucous as they sip
from glistening blades
Mustafah, grey tomcat sits
regal beggar awaiting
free-fall breakfast

and I, a prisoner, luxuriate
wealthy in morning light
wrapped in this anywhere world tableau

guards' voices clang
the last drops of bitter coffee
nudge my lips into resolution
Mustafah flees
Sunday becomes prison

AIR NIKE SLAM DUNK

Vietnamese women
forced to work
65 hours per week
for 10 dollars
no time for

basketball games

ALARMS

on a shady porch with Geronimo
yeah, free Geronimo
others there too
like we said we'd do
once we were free
dream state delight
does not come often
my lips must be curved
in night-draped smiles

fire alarm screams me awake
scratches at my eyes
snatches my dream
my cellmate leans down
what should we do

yanked from other world communication
I mutter
why get up
no way out
no one coming
go back to sleep Grace

and turn over
dream-searching

gone
lost in prison night blare

WOMAN'S JAZZ BAND PERFORMS AT WOMEN'S PRISON

on a sad childless street
tears rain down in gutters
where not even trash twists
in long-absent winds
the blues stay indoors
too drained to wait
only lipstick-stained butts
betray women presence

trombone slides around the corner
of this torn-down town
she dares to disturb
shuttered discontent
and calls down winds
subversive

from an abandoned doorway
where she's saved up the news
sax steps out to wander
intentional behind trombone
floats afro blue on green
dolphin street along route 66
and blows "a song for my father"
or mother

momma bass breaks from behind
grey-laced shadows
shrugs 'cause drum's detained
scats
wake up women
take down the drab

keyboard skitters *yeah*
walks her bass between
cracks kicking down doors
keys reign supreme
prisoners stir
from catacombs of muzak misery

A 1950'S GIRL THINKS ABOUT LOVE
ON A SWELTERING SUMMER DAY

your love would be
like popping the cap off
a green-glass Coke bottle
frosty cold sweaty
from the ice chest
at the Mojave desert last stop
filling station

CHRISTIAN CHARITY

D. Nix testifies about the murder of
J. Dahmer thirty years later

Deavours Nix joined the Klan
he says because they were
a bunch of benevolent Mississippi boys
known for their Christmas baskets
full of firebomb oranges
      fruitcake beatings
      cranberry ropes
      and cracked nuts

accompanied by a cross

JASPER, TX

in memory of James Byrd, Jr.

1958
Saturday bare feet dusted red
on East Texas roads
shrieks slice heavy summer air
white children play
fearless in pine-shadowed lanes
till darkfall
we're called in
behind screen doors

Sunday sermons spill
out windows
in sticky heat our washed feet
bound in oxfords
& patent leather swing
while ladies in flower-print dresses
bob hats perched on dishwater curls
in prayer to God . . .
some other God?
than the one down the road
in churches where Black families
pray for deliverance
from nights of crossburnings
or lynchings
amen

1998
Pine-drenched night
once barefoot white killer-boys
play Drag-a-Black-Man
tear sleepy red roads awake
with dusty devils of terror
behind their pick-up
James Byrd's bound feet carve
a bloody ribbon
his screams cut off
by the lynching chain
dancing in the dirt

James Byrd could not
get behind a screen door
in time

RESCUE THE WORD

sacred words are in danger
fugitives, they seek cover
bury themselves alive
shamed by the profane
purposes they are forced to serve
dressed in lily-white lies

words are in danger
english only vows
to tear out tongues
exiled witnesses
to collective memory and homeland

sacred words are in danger
trapped, they hang on billboards
judas-goats to conjure deception

sing them shout them
teach them
wear them
around your neck
amulets against amnesia

BACKLIT

the telephone rings
I await connection
my eyes cruise the tier
rest on Lupe, backlit
   she stands as if unseen
      except by herself
   before the mirror

her arms unfurl upward
electric bronze hands poised
   sail down serpentine
      smooth cherry-streaked tresses
   slide down slowly
      to linger then on breasts
         sequestered from lover's lips

languorous she sighs
wraps her shoulders
in solaced embrace
   she shudders
   hands fall

         empty

Lupe turns back
   into the shadows

I turn to *hello* in my ear
my eyes flicker back
   Lupe steps out pressed
      into another khaki-clad day

PRISON CHANT

Cassandra is on the phone
her screams bounce off walls
staccato chant

jesusfathergod
jesusfathergod
Maurice listen to me
Stop   listen to me
listen
listen
you must be responsible
I'm not there
take care of your sister
help her
I don't care
she's young
you're grown
20 is grown
I'm sorry you must
be responsible
I'm not there

Let me talk to her
LISA   LISA
jesusfathergod
Stop

listen to me
listen to your brother
TIME OUT
what's going on
Stop   STOP   STOP
jesusfathergod
I'm sorry

no the phone has cut me off
I need more time
please let me call again
I know you're next
please
please jesusfathergod
I must call back
I'm going to call again
I know it's your turn
you have to wait

Maurice I'm sorry
I'm not there
what can I do
I know your brother's dead
yes I told
I had to
to come home
yes I'm still here
you're there
you're alive

you must be responsible
I'm not there
I'm still not there
jesusfathergod
jesusfathergod

DEFINITION

when I was much younger
than I am now
my mom told me
look out for tall dark strangers
I thought she meant
look for one

OUR GIANT

brooding Irish Atlas
props long-legged baby
in the window of a '47 car
(a car I remember better
than my father's sweet attentions)
the only clue left of kindness
     a bled-orange Kodacolor

a handsome rundown football player
like a thundering giant
he dangled our lives from his fingertips
   four morsels
we hovered over the chasm of his rage
our tears seasoned his wounds
swallowed whole
   we were regurgitated
     each daybreak

we ate the scraps
   of his bitterness
we swallowed his grief

skittish shades we scattered
   in the sunlight
we ran, pushed back
   the one behind

only when our ogre left to roar
    at wrongs
did our tip-toes touch down

(we didn't know
he was pursued by demons
    too)

he was our giant, defrocked
he stomped in "jesus sandals"
stained the silken robes
    of rich men's hypocrisy
a jeremiah in farmboy overalls
    and starched Mexican wedding shirt

titanic storms flayed his flesh
too angry to leave this too-small world
he finally found a way to ask
    permission to end
    his frenzied flagellation
when at last, he realized
he was loved

WILD POPPIES

I remember red poppies, wild behind the school house
I didn't want to be there, but I loved to watch the
poppies

I used to sit in the window of my room, sketching
charcoal trees
what happened to those magnolia trees, to that girl?

I went off to college, escaped my father's thunderstorms
Berkeley. Rebellion. Exhilaration!

the Vietnam war, Black Power, Che took me to Chicago
midnight lights under Wacker Drive. Uptown. South
Side. slapped
by self-determination for taking Freedom Wall photos
without asking

on to California, driving at 3:00 in the morning in the
mountains
I got it: what self-determination means
a daunting task for a young white woman, I was humbled

practice is concrete . . . harder than crystal-dream
concepts

San Francisco, on the front steps at Fulton Street
smoking reefer, drinking "bitterdog" with Black Panthers
    and white
hippie radicals, talking about when the revolution comes

the revolution did not come. Fred Bennett was missing
we learned he'd been found: ashes, bones, a wedding ring
but later there was Assata's freedom smile

then I was captured, locked into a cell of sewer water
spirit deflated. I survived, carried on, glad to be
like a weed, a wild red poppy
rooted in life

PHOTO MEMORY RECALL

September 2001 a 1973 photo
   sepia on New York Times page
men stand in National Stadium
   in shirt sleeves, light jackets
      they look out
captured in the camera's eye

another man stands in the foreground
before the fence
in fatigues
   rifle ready
      on guard
a helmet hides his face
he looks away from the camera

among the 16 prisoners
fixed in September's sights
Aguero at least survived
he remembers
he remembers a face
across the decades
         a face
across a Miami room
     a torturer's face
   Prof. Meneses' face

indignant
   Meneses denies
   I was there but I knew

                  nothing

   I am innocent I knew

                  nothing

   I call on innocence

             and law

16 prisoners and thousands more
could not call on innocence
   or law
innocence was tortured
   bled over that Chilean spring
   disappeared into unmarked graves
     executed by military scientists
       their recall now dim
         and disingenuous

HALLUCINATION

exhilaration sticks in her throat
she stands still, water to her knees
warm waves lap
a pack of dogs hunting for sunrise
beyond moon tides

close your eyes
hum seven circles of hyacinths
around carnation's blush
arise a black dahlia
mu li shah sha
she ro shah mu
ring bells, light incense
warm the water with your breath
let your tongue swim with words
as they scatter the moments
   petals on fool's gold

BOSTON POST ROAD BLUES

from a Boston Post Roadhouse
music probes the velcro night
through swinging doors and scuffling soles
throbbing light reveals a corner sentry,
      awaiting calls for help
      a drunkard's *babyplease*
      letmecome home
        or someone like me

I wait in the car's darkness I count
minutes and coins
      11:00 I step through blinking neon
      into the vacant booth drop coins
      and hear a click

the plum-colored voice
      Baby, I'm here
trumpet notes tap along my spine
my delight a waterfall
      blues turn bold
        intimate in the dark

click, the coins run out
the music of his voice cuts off
      I walk out into blue notes

in daylight I drive down Boston Post Road
the blues house stands blank
bone dry and noiseless

THE OWL

Emma woman needed no serpent
   to know the ways of the world
she whirled around, looked down on nakedness
   and approved
perched upon the apple branch, fist clenched
she whooped
   why listen
      to a snake when one is

a perspicacious owl
   spectacled, panoramic eyes penetrating
   penumbras of hybrid white mice pretending
   to be blue-blood swans?

Emma owl swooped
arched wings and ruffled feathers
emanated storms:
   red & black   worker ants sallied
   from rattletrap tenements
   mine shafts and foundry furnaces
      you have nothing

to lose but your chains
   they marched uptown
      to strike

the swindle-starched underbellies
of gold-dust-whiskered rats

aria-throated plebian owl she
    flew   flew
indefatigable over seas and land
wings fanning freedom

READING POETRY

Chao Ut reads Vietnamese poetry
I tell her she reads well
she smiles

    my mother and father
        used to nap
        in the afternoons
    they always said
        Gai Ut, read to us
    they liked me to read
        in those days when
        I was a young girl
            in Vietnam

she reads another poem
        it sounds like music, I say
    yes, I'll read it again
        the way we everyday talk
she reads
        do you hear?
            yes, I say

    some people read poetry
        some can't so well
        yes, I say
Ut and I, we smile.

17th PARALLEL

Marceline has numbers
tattooed along her arm
remembrance of teenage internment
she survived Auschwitz at 18
in '73 she arrived in Vietnam
    to document this other war
    the American war
she wished to travel to the 17th parallel
and waited permission with her husband
Pham Van Dong told her
    no, it's too dangerous
    for a woman so small

the sound of slippered feet
on former French salon floors
turned her head
Ho Chi Minh stood there
introduced, Ho saw
the numbers on her arm
    if you were not fried
    and did not die
    yes, you can go
    to the 17th parallel

LOSS

my mother died at 74
I believed she would
   no, should live till 80

she was supposed to live till 80
so I could live till 80
so I would make it out of prison
   alive

   my supposition
   stares back at me
      ashes

my mother's anger
swam in blue-water eyes
a grief she did not want to bear
   her daughter
   imprisoned
   an enemy of the state

   she could not save me
   from vengeful-suited men
      nor from myself

her anger etched itself
onto my dark eyes
and dissolved in drops of sorrow
   between us

GRAFFITI

for Salim Elijah

rapping artists
paint outside the margins
replace the page
    ad absurdo   ad reductio
in the face of linewatchers
margins bleed
       on center stage

fingerprints rage
on perpendiculars
   secret language
   survival codes
hip-hop-hope

murals relieve
   ad-riddled wastelands
wipe out decorum
vibrate acrylic screams
project the unadult
   aerated

in one thousand years
   disinterred from millennial dirt

a wall may bare its breast
    spray-paint hieroglyphs
for future archeologists
to decipher

"PERCHANCE TO DREAM"

night comes
i fall exhausted into sleep
   i dream of Dresden   Hanoi   Baghdad
      whistles scream
      walls fall apart
        in waves
     Dali deserts
       watches tick
         waterdrip

   dream shift:
      swords of steel glint against the sky
      a swarm and puff
      dark blood drops
      bituminous birds bank
      spread-eagled free fall
      ashes ashes they all fall
        down dark flashes
      cherry splashes on concrete
      Babel towers collapse in crying heaps
      a curtain rises gray
      covers gladiators draped across the stage

i wake cold-throated
what time is it?

my limbs locked
beneath a concrete rockslide
is this my tomb falling on me?

my chest is piled rock-heavy
    bodies rise from the shallows of my breath
 graze my eyes and flee
       across the desert scape
         shadow prints dissipate
am i awake?

the Cyclops stabs my eye
    i must be awake
i wrap a scratchy towel
around my face
i escape electric night
    into sightlessness

a ghost voice wails
    what time is it?
a deep male boom
       1:24, go to sleep
       no, turn on the radio, talk to me
no! no! please no, my eyes blink
inside their blind
    little Brueghel men dance
    wooden-shoe notes
    ruthless on my sleep

sound streams woman's babble
pools beneath the door
i hunker under the winding sheet

does she stop talking
or do i descend?
i don't remember

    shift change
        shift change
guards come and go
officials pass by peering
    into our crypt-cages
    taking notes, verifying

SUNFALL

a purple eyelash swallows
the withering sun, flutters
on the velvet swing
brushes exhilarated flames
across the creep of rosy rises
breath buttered with anticipose
waterbraced by empation
impatiens for an apertif
purcress to dream conjunctions
on the backs of bird's cous
cous concantenations insinuate
red below bare-breast peaks
mango sandia zabayone

21ST & GUERRERO: 1968

on 21st and Guerrero we lounge in the kitchen
the soldier stands smoking hash beside the fridge

smoke curls latakia fragrant, fades above our heads
Aretha raises ariatic storms from the front room

Annie calls from down the hall, "baby, come here"
the curtains hang lacy, defenseless before the fog

no one speaks, laughter works its way into lapses
the soldier drops solid, hit by pipe dreams. we stop

laughing. "wake up!" the sun scatters through the fog
I shiver in fugitive light

REVELATION

This is a time when the world seeks revelation.
Too many seek that which is not but illusion or reassurance;
those who thirst for visions drink hallucinations.

the future perfect tense belongs to charlatans; pied pipers
lead the future into deceptions poisoned seas.
      cataclysms, punishments, hell, damnation,
      all mirages of souls in anguish
      salvation for the elect: they fear
      themselves and the echoes of mountain tombs.

Do you see demons and desolation, hear sounds
of screams, wailing? Or smell sulfur burn
behind your tongue — a taste of wormwood
and aloes? Or encounter the touch as a torch upon the skin?
      You imagine fire but it might be ice.

Hounds of hell,
horse's pounding hooves are ancient;
they tread through all the tales.

    Children who do not ripen on the vine cling and hide
beneath the bitter leaves, composting hatred of the world:
    their ear is stopped to the sweet sounds of Ascension
blown by Tranes of quotidian toilers, artists of the
      ordinary;

their eye shuts before the flesh of their own desire,
they name it decadence — hell for defiant revelers;
    they singe the air with sanctimony and light bonfires
        beneath
the feet of non-conformity (flaming lovers deserts for
    mordant palates)
    demons race upon their tongue, salty
toads, ready to leap into hyssop-broomed allegories.
    They reproach those who dare lay among the lilies of
        the field.

Do you see the light that flirts on willow leaves
fallen in the stream? Do you hear the universe
sounding in a Robeson basso tremor? Or smell
the fragrance of the unsought kiss? Or cry
when the moon washes silken on your skin?
Do you taste dandelions dressed in orange and olive's coat?

For you, no religious processionals
apocalypse no final reckoning:
    the day discovers itself, opens opal prospects,
    sweat drops from the brow, a stream mysterious
     unto itself.
        red is vermilion, green is emerald
        commingled dissolution
        into mud, the prism flawed by the acid mire
        of doomsday incantations.

All you do not know is of a different globe.
Rejoice! You will not go there; you circle not that realm.

Ignore false prophets, find mysteries for yourself
apocalyptic chanters sing sadomasochistic
fantasies for those who live on surfaces and beg for fancy
    trinkets
fanciful proof of perfect spirit.

Calamity follows the radiant day:
would you know stillness without the roiling of the seas?

You shall glimpse that you do not know
in the sound of the cedars in the night
and children weeping; in the smell of the rain
and taste of drought, in the breath of longing
upon your breast, and in the sight of bodies
strewn across ravished landscapes.

Do not be blind to the longitudes of the world:
embrace the latitudes and all they offer
    disown fear to live tomorrow.

Seek not revelations, all is revealed.
Listen to each word, a world in orbit;
each phrase, a nova: essay the beach,
each grain of sand, a poem

        do not sit idle, your path streams before you.
        bank the raging fires and light laurel branches
            against the cold

FRIDAY, 13 SEPTEMBER 2002

I stroll into the visiting room
      smiles, embraces
Felix asks how I am
cool, I say
      a Sylvia Plath day
early, middle, late?
          late, I say
          but maybe
             not

LET ME RAMBLE

let me ramble here
yet stay within the yardlines
no   let me trespass beyond
          (the bounds are tight
          they slice like knives
          beneath the lights)

I've been sidelined too long
my knees creak

I'll stay beyond the lines
smudge them with my toes

the portals are not
as substantial as they used to be

I lean down
        with creaking knees
look through a macro lens
        rusty tracks and cracks
on doors and lines appear

POSTCARDS

mail call begins: 4:30 pm
uncommon precision
in this regimented jail

my name is called and called
again until at the end
the last piece is called
it's mine

        a postcard straight

I read the backs while standing
and spread my hand:
the gallery opens

ashen chili peppers piled into a pyre
on pale desert sands
tongue sticks out alabaster

above a wide opened third eye
a mammoth beetle's pod
hauled here from a Jurassic age
Burning Man rite 2001

fanning out: a Pacific Northwest
mural across a wall
eyes and mouths peer out

seals and birds and whales
red and green on ochred wood
wrapped black soft-edged universes

my eyes pass on to harsher borders
a kaffiyeh, black and white dissolves
into barbed-wire projections
slashing Palestinian homeland

into ribbons

then, red blood drops
on parchment skin, Eastern poppies,
". . . distinguished by the splendor
of their colors," black velvet eyes
encompass pregnant heart

and last, O'Keefe's "Cottonwood Tree
in Spring" alizarin branches, a Tilt-a-Whirl
axis of yellow feathers silver-veined

spinning to the edge
to push the splintered sky
into superfluity

the hand is done

UNTITLED

*"I have been in many shapes before I
attained congenial form"*

Lew Welch

once, I was a rock
a broken bit of Nature's force
ground down into a seed,
      a grain that found its way
into a prowling oyster
      I took shape
a pearl rough but smoothing
      out by years

I keep taking shapes
congenial or not
    depends
on circumstance

THROUGH A CIRCLE

a circle, circumscribed
          by time and distance
beyond the prison wire

      the circle's edge rolls
a hoop across the roil
         of concertina wire
         scalpel-sharp steel slivers
perforate the border

      a tangent rises alongside
weather-dulled metal pole
      its top intrudes,
      drops a half-lidded eyeball
      inside, a white grape hanging blank
until sunset when its glare whites out
      all circles,
      opening them to scrutiny

      framed, a tall pineapple-skinned palm
slices off an arc
      frowsy fronds hang exhausted
        by fumes
        spewed by black ants scurrying
along a concrete slash
      across my eye

beyond, urine fog blurs
horizontal waves of hay-parched hills
the only relief evergreen ridges

and far beyond, the bleached-blue sky
spreads
indescribable absence

GUERRILLA GRRL

I am guerrilla grrl
no capital gs nor
tongue in cheek apes
baboons or monkeys
more like an owl
whrring in deep
shadows. well
why are you here
now

          at this place
guerrillas are unacceptable
these days; why
do you hesitate in speaking
here now at this place
these days

everything is conditional
in this place
of the dismissed
unpleasantly so
I might add, I suggest
you look down
          at your feet

confirm yourself

a name, you mean
this place I mean
you. I have a name
you don't   if you did
you'd know the name
            of the concrete place
all conditionals would be
conditioned

predicated.
guerrilla grrl, may
I call you that? only
on the condition
you call yourself
            without hesitation

my name is
            Dorothy

finally.
of the shoes?
no, I once had shoes but now
again the conditional
no the story
what happened? I lost my shoes
on the flight I never had
shoes myself
acrobats need no shoes

             we swing
across streets
like monkeys? to slip
into alleys of unconsciousness

why do you seek
unconscious states? not
states, alleys
learn to be precise

since you're so
interested in precision
how does a guerilla grrl
get to be
an acrobat

not *a, we.* we? there must be
more than one to catch me
in mid-air
             training, training?
that's the point, the intersection
                        precise indeed

to clarify, not accuracy
such lies beyond reach beyond
the point. it leaves no room
for doubt
boring, we agree

we do? what do we agree to?
      dangling prepositions

of course, for that
you need an acrobat

GUERRILLA GRRL II

let's look for a bar then
now would be better
            guerrilla grrl strides ahead
her legs look longer
than they could possibly be
perhaps it's the black jeans
why do you question my legs?
how do you know what I'm thinking?
streams of consciousness my legs are
long enough to cross cracks in the sidewalks
of convention they wrap around
          the trapeze with ease
will your legs extend beyond
frontiers? I have no frontiers
only boundaries. no, frontiers,
you are the Dot

like a period at the end
of a sentence?
no, the center of the circle
you imagine you're stuck inside
a drying cycle

I'm dry that's true
my skin's like dust
on Granddad's concertina

        soundless in the basement
a Dot begins the vector
arrows in all directions
for your bow
to puncture
        frontiers
are to be crossed
preferably on a trapeze
I'm not sure about this flying
fear of flying leads
to dying let's
        have a drink
oh that bar not
a trapeze
of course it is
it's a start, follow me

centrifugal, GG splits
in two, a G-force fugue
ensues catches
the Dot
we swing, wet with
expectation, dauntless

my ears ring looking back
I see my shoes bronzed
I thought I'd lost these let's
stop no your shoes are

a brass ring, a noose
to encircle Dot

I shrug loss is the cost
of breaking out we cross
a stream of consciousness
refugees from propriety

ESPERANZA'S BODY

Lies buried beneath
ancient sands
casualty of war
across the world
> women winds
> bear culture cross
> *hermanas*

mothers and sisters
sweep the earth
fresh with spring branches

COUNTERWEIGHTS

1.
middle of time flight
men stand
    in awe
    dazzled
        by the speed of travel
    not yet light years
    but more lights
        than ever before
reach
    out to whirligigs
    of words
find fragments
    to express
what's happening
    at the time
        it's happening

hyperstimulated
    nerves frazzle
        thirst for more
    fear flourishes
        as entertainment

shocks kinesthetic
roller coasters
    moving pictures
mood swings
    in tangled webs
        nylon networks
spin round heads
    of workers
        and dreamers

gone crazy
mutating
    synchronizing into
    mechanical mankind
        in radical rush
    of distance crushed
        into time
clocks punch
    holes in perceptions
boredom
    assuaged by aesthetics
        of astonishment
addictions
    feed spider man
        swinging through
        disconnected consciousness

sci-fi big heads
    neuronal nirvana
        or
do dendrites die
from lack
    of more and more

2.
trauma transforms
    postmodern childminds
no need for knowledge
when google rules
    rearchitects   constructs
no need to detect
cyberworld's
    time/space collapse
        binary biorhythms
    into   screen dancers
digital divas jackknife
    between
        virtual screens
    fingered by keys and
    umbilical chord operations

ad art pares neuronal perception
    into bytes
    nanosecond revelations

necromanticized bodies
  bleed across
  cinematic pupils
ADHD babies
    pixilate
beyond their wildest imaginations

Shirley's "Cool World"
  mutates into icicle light show
MTV stabs conscience
  in the eye

3.
unscreened worlds
look up
  at flying fragmentation
    bombs
not yet postmodern
  turn collective aim
  toward other possibilities

weave desire from webs
  left behind in caves of consciousness

BEAR WITNESS

sing a song that rushes unafraid against
desert storms
      or

start a chant that abets the waves
of inhabitants dispossessed

stir a dirge that drives out men of ill
      intentions

breathe inside the silence
      whistling through still-bleeding bones

in these times such sounds are all
the ears can bear as witness

WORLD AIDS DAY 1998

for Princess

I dreamt of dancing
to leap around arpeggios and drums
       Princess knew my dreams
       her dancer's rhythm broken too
       feet caught by traps and symbols

she landed barefoot beside me
suspended between the bars
she shook off regret
       swept the floor with grace notes

Princess drew me there
made me dance despite
a mangled leg
       I can't
       you shall

imperious
she choreographed my steps
beside her own
I slid and turned
she leapt and whirled
       a pause   a glide

we danced dreams
across the floor
  in memoriam
to those who died
and living still

SENSE OF SUBSTANCE

Lapsang souchong tea in china
teacups catch glints of light
incensed ribbons weave
      between us across worn wood
Nina Simone sings Pernod melodies
walls thrum with black-berried attitude
our murmurs brush behind the ivoried beats

my lips reach to taste smoked dark liquid
      kiss of substance

INSIDE SHADOWS

I love your shadow across the sun
drown the laughter of the loveless
darken the alleys of the sentries
pull me from the glare of spotlights

I love the light inside your shadow
lead me through the glass-strewn streets
hold my hand across the razored rivers
keep my heart from frozen lakes

wrap your shadow round my shoulders
fade me into the darkness beyond
              hunters' eyes

THE WHIP

For B.W.

a strawberry blonde woman
      sits
on a bench,   the evening dusk
      sits on the wire
          behind her lover

his hands cross
      the space
of absence   to caress
Rapunzel's locks
      a remembered benediction
twilight's breath shimmers lilac
beyond the touch
      a blessing kiss   on upturned brow
         reverence holds the light still

a white shirt cracks the light
      beside my eye
the spike-haired guard stands
      voice whips out
raps Rapunzel's back
         her finger orders   "come *here*"

she stands and turns
      light leaks from her hair

she walks,   a wraith shrinking inside her cloak
furious whispering cuts the becalmed eve

the prisoner returns to her love
        jaw line taut
        iridescence stripped

at visit's end
she and he stand
        face to face
        eight inches space

unreachable
once more the whip cracks
"all visitors to this side
                inmates over there
        now"

a merciless farewell

EXORCISM

the healer reaches
into her   encounters
        the alien
in her stomach which
    before she could not
        stomach those
           unlike her

"LOVE SUPREME" WEEKEND

"love supreme" blows
 through the bars
penetrates anesthetized loss

notes rain on the air
rare blue bird's wings flash
on wintered branches
in the corner of my eye

ii

topdog/underdog
idles before the light
turns green
foot on the pedal
revving
smooth   man

glances to the side
men strolling
scope women hip rolls
can't help themselves
the women stride, fixed
on the grocery store
at the corner

light goes green
eight-horse-leap forward
horns tap
at women's backs
they keep on
          walking

past stoops of children
swooping down back beats
in the streets
open-lidded windows flutter
colored flags out to dry
on half-note breezes

metal clashes
the cat in the doorway
scopes a chase
into the alley   copper
throws young blood
against bare brick wall
cans cymbal   bounce
off the grate
soprano screams
wind wraps youngblood
kisses sticky red
off his face
whispers revival

CONTINUUM

stocks and bonds tied tight
public dunkings and drownings
massacres and land grabs
Indian scalps   Vietnamese
ears on belts posed in
front of tiger cages
shackles and manacles
whips across African backs
chained in darkness below decks
boiled in oil tendons cut
for fleeing from the terror
genitals ripped   lynchings
rape sanctioned under law
children sold further South
collective punishment
solitary confinement
food mixed with piss
pushed through metal door slots
four-pointed bodies on steel slabs
paraded naked, testicles twisted
only urine to drink are you
thirsty yet
electrified cattle prods
alligator clips on eyelids
on vaginal lips
restraint chairs strung up by arms

isolated
in the dark   in the light
no sleep   deprived of diurnal rhythm
humiliated, beaten bloodied
accidental death

forced to tell a story constructed
by the captors

the secrets behind the American dream
democracy behind steel-bolted

doors. Inquisition never sleeps
its eyes probe with laser
beams of national security
and manifest destiny

DELIRIUM III

Silence is golden
shut up
listen to the clang of its mettle

BLAKE'S MILTON: POETIC
APOCALYPSE (selections)

"TIME IS THE MERCY OF ETERNITY?"

Cast into iron-bound panopticon – Ulro's labyrinth;
even the wind drifts forlorn inside the howls of tyranny;
leeway's salve smeared into shadows behind solid bars:
in depths of mourning, doves coo silent.
The poet falters before ratio's rule, the certitude of
    punishment
relentless; ferrous-toothed grins bolt all without its
    boundaries.
Fire extinguishes, shrunken cold inside the ivory-carved
    vault,
forgotten; a shadow of itself; outside
spheres of patriarchal apprehension, dread materializes
a jealous guardian imposing limits:

Contraction's boundaries defined by twisted tongues
Counted. Numbered. beings weep
wail for release from temporal habitation;
memory dances in seven veils, swaddling oblivion's
    cocoon.

Fall: the poet turns in sodden space, an oceanic whirlpool
swallows, sea-washed sands seal her mouth,
into dunes of silence: fractionated, Space holds time

like a deformed twin, Satan's tyranny,
poet space suspends from weaver's web
within the sentence. She loses the point in Time's endless
    deceptions,
imagined a sword. Fragments break icebergs off the floe.
Tharmic seas swell – a salted tongue.

The poet twists inside fractal's generations,
dazzling kaleidoscopic flashes
in the dark, regeneration' possibility.

POET'S SLEEP

Queried consciousness, measured length and breadth:
too much sleep with eagles, swallowed into Eternal death
Liberty lies asleep upon retinal couches.

The poet rocks between sleep of heights and depths
a stupor upon a sheet, the world unfurled
upon a couch of tattered expectation,
stretched between the poles of transparencies

Blind-sighted, she sees the liberation road, long
overgrown by wrathful nettles. Though she'd sung
    Liberty's song
its tones rang organ-grinder tinny, rusted in cacophony's
    sea.

Dharmic tears drop on the poet's tongue; sweet waters
    return
Waking between breaths, inspired space incites:
the pen pierces the poles.

POET'S CHALLENGE

An idol on the alter of conception: "progress"
banishes Eternal knowledge to the altar cloth
names feeling as the whole never as the singular
And behind the altar, Perception's door guarded
by covering cherubs, they mask the written line
in opaque purity where liberation is a sacrament; and
    bread
for the Elect. They drink passion purples, furious reds,
    set upon
reason's tapestry, illusions derived by deft magicians with
    lead wires.

Imagine beyond the sentence:
breathe dimensions into the flattened grass of the senses:
compression, and expansion, affirm resistance to
    collapse.
Doors open out from straitened lines of experience,
    imposed
order shatters; citizens are not in the streets to witness
what has happened

The shards do not fit, the mosaic will.

JERUE'S ASYLUM

On the day Jerue considered
the fourth and fifth sense, the clock stopped in Eternity,
wild thyme's scent blew as
Ella's note shattered glass ceilings;
the mundane moment stretched
as fire sang through the winds,
the horn spun golden.

Illumination; error scatters in shadowed motes.

ARISEN LOGOS

Underground: the world of dreams illuminates
sparkling the poet whirls
among bimbé dancers, intoxicated with amplification
she falls through the pit in spiral clarification;
music reaches copper-toned to fill the expanse
at the borders of her day, Beulah's trumpets
pierce memory's dreaming eye
flashes through the fingers; sound waves seed
the fertile field, and earthy fragrance flutters like
        dandelions.

Trumpets sound, each upon a note
swirling outward from the musical octave
she looks into the flower of its annunciation

a cochlear spiral into the sound
gusts of wind hold notes swirling from center
simultaneous chords alight.

The poet breathes burning bushes,
incense of fallen leaves;
the sweet waters of destination
reach the border lands,
passport written in her eyes.

CROSSINGS

For Miranda

1. In the midst of everything
death enters, like a whirlwind beyond
the speed limit set by my natural laws

2. Swept in the wake
I cry out *wait*
come back, get off the ferry!
it's not a day trip
your slackening breath inverts the sails
the wind can't push back

3. Standing, quayside
pebbles in my shoes
I hold the anchor, the fraying rope
strains against my efforts

4. I quarry
stone shards of secrets
clasped within our fists:
      we're fakirs who never feared crossings,
        roads winding through the sage
      we carried our patient stones of woe
      lightly   lightly

5. I did not know
these patient stones would gather
into a grave remembrance

FIXED

The ghost that runs before your eyes
buries bodies, scatters
stardust, a path
out of ruined woods into absence
no chirps and leaf clatters

it's the fixer man
he pushes, shoves you into red velvet seats
to watch the show instead of trimming trees

he's God's under-hand man
prestidigitator adman
illusions popup through pixels
pour into irises
rabbits leap from hats
unknown to undergrowth
no wild black berries
beneath the rhododendron

the sawed lady doesn't die
anorexic, skin and bone
faced with cornucopias of food
she throws up heads in baskets
exotic coconuts
island pineapples

rust-gilt smoke streams from trains
smothers temples

hold your breath before
you go up in smoke
demolecularized by shiny uranium
knife throwers

the fixer fixes all
even though you didn't know
something was broken

lobotomized, you may smile now.

HUNGRY

the alligator opens mouth, inhales its dinner
minnows, trout, at times whole mammals:
hunger's fatalities

a void appears in the food chain
minnows and higher up work hard to fill
for people it's more difficult
who will buy the groceries now?

BLUE HERON

I, splendid by design, see myself in my silhouette
on the earth, and in the mirror
of your eyes, a breath of loveliness,
my blue fades to gray, reflects late day's sky
the fluffy white cloud of my belly floats lazy
under wings feathered lace in the winds: I sail

you revel in my exquisiteness, until:
you grasp why I light so still
in radiant light: I do not move
though winds tickle my feathered crown
still, still: I hunt

to feed my hatchlings
hungry, hidden, not yet grand
enough to fly or please your eye

Silent, I stand calculating:
the fall of my shadow
(it never betrays my presence)
the distance of my beak,
the speed with which this warrior spear will thrust
into tiny ground squirrels huddling in earthen nest

a statue, poised, until
a hapless little morsel grows impatient

or bold, hungry for sweet green blades,
singing edibles in the wind

I strike, I stab
my beak trickles ruby lace
on my ruffled white breast
my babies need to eat, to fly

I swallow, you cry
revulsion blushing your face,
such an exquisite bird, how ghastly!
I spoil your bird watching idyll
the wind blows dust into your eye

BIRDS ON A WIRE

we wait in a line
we wait our turn
we wait to do yoga
we wait to work out
we wait to run around the track
we wait to pass through
the metal detector, a squawking sentinel
inside Recreation's close, shadowy entrance

we move forward, one by one
as the morning settles in upon the sunrise

above, birds rustle
winged brushes upon sparkling air
the starlings line up
along the wire radians stretching out high above
anti-helicopter guards

birds stream from night time perches in thirsty trees
an early morning assemblage
silhouettes sail and light upon the wires
bird lines elongate, birds jostle for position
some flit to other lines, insinuate themselves
they chirp and chatter, an indignant squawk
from one that does not
concede its place

a game of musical chairs,
bird rules of engagement

forward, my turn
I pass into the noisy gloom
pass through inspection's maw
raucous squawking red light
     Step aside!
my knee, you know
     Okay, go!

NO LOVE POEM

I wake, eyes open to what must
be a new day, creeping across the dark
I turn to the wall to the emptiness
no lover fills my eyes

across a narrow passage, only a reach away
rising from the fading shades,
yellow interior shadows
white-blanketed shapes, two, bunked
one above the other

they too lie, waiting to open eyes
against all desire
to their own empty beds

THE FIRST YEAR YOU LEARN TO WEAR
THE ROBES

Alan, the Buddhist priest opens his dharma talk with
    words
his teacher told him on stepping into the Zen priesthood

to wrap one robe and then another, is not so simple as it
    looks
rather this is not a simple matter of getting dressed, not
    a covering
a process of finding oneself inside one's situation,
revelation

a prisoner must learn to wear robes of absence
prepared to live this day

ACKNOWLEDGMENTS

Editor's Note: Marilyn Buck wrote these acknowledgments before the book was edited for publication, which took place after her death. We include them here, the way she wrote them, in order to thank those she intended to thank at that time.

I wasn't much of a poetry lover until I ran smack dab into Nikki Giovanni, Sonia Sanchez, June Jordan and Alice Walker in the 1960s. The power of these Black women and other audacious, determined liberation-minded women made the poetic real: the spirit, the passion, the word. I didn't imagine myself as a poet until I read Mitsuye Yamada's *Camp Notes*. She continues to encourage me.

Without the vision of justice and human liberation that have embraced me and freed my imagination, my words would never have become poetry. And if it weren't for so many friends, comrades and supporters this book would not have been possible. Special thanks to Felix Shafer, Miranda Bergman, Raul Salinas and David Meltzer, who dreamed this book with me and made it possible. Thanks to Tom Parsons and Graciela Trevisan, and to all the constant Friends of Marilyn Buck from San Francisco to New York who have helped to get my words into the world. And thank you Penny Schoner for all your patience in typing up all my writings, not once but multiple times.

Finally I thank all who struggle for a day, for a year, for a lifetime.

Printed in the USA
CPSIA information can be obtained
at www.ICGtesting.com
JSHW082220140824
68134JS00015B/634

9 780872 865778